WORKERS COMPENSATION

THE FIRST ONE HUNDRED YEARS

CERTIFICATION PROGRAM

WCP®

COURSE GUIDE

Copyright © AMCOMP 2011
Third Edition 2015
The American Society of Workers Comp Professionals, Inc.

Acknowledgements

Many people have shared their advice and information in developing the text and Course Guide covering the broad aspects of the workers compensation program which is greatly appreciated. The authors would especially like to acknowledge the Board of Directors of AMCOMP for their support and advice throughout the process.

A special thank you is extended to Lucy DeCaro Vice President of Operations of the New York Workers Compensation Insurance Rating Board for her countless hours reviewing and editing the material covered in both the text and Course Guide along with John Leonard, President of the Maine Employers Mutual Insurance Company (MEMIC) who devoted valuable time and provided valuable services of the members of his staff to review and comment on the text. Their input has been invaluable in producing the current edition of the text.

Special thanks is also extended to Dr. Peter Barth, retired economics professor at the University of Connecticut; Warren Heck, former Chairman and CEO of GNY Insurance Companies; Richard W. Palczynski, principal and founder of Sea Tower Insurance Consulting; Mike Stinziano, chair of the AMCOMP Education Committee and Senior Vice President of Demotech, Inc.; Greg Krohm, former Executive Director of the International Association of Industrial Accident Boards and Commissions (IAIABC); Bonnie Piacentino, Vice President Pennsylvania/Delaware Compensation Rating Bureau; Carole Banfield, independent consultant; and to many others who have provided their input, suggestions and chapter reviews that are so important to the project.

We would also like to extend our thanks to Donna Oxford, Executive Director of AMCOMP along with the members from Accolade Management Services for their continued support and guidance. Only through the support and direction of these and many more individuals have we been able to accomplish this huge task.

About the Authors

Donald T. DeCarlo, Esq., WCP

Donald T. DeCarlo, Esq. is the principal of an independent law firm in Lake Success, NY, which focuses on mediation/arbitration and regulatory and insurance counseling. Before establishing the firm in 2005, Mr. DeCarlo was a Partner at Lord Bissell & Brook LLP and headed its New York office. Formerly, he was Senior Vice President and General Counsel of The Travelers Insurance Companies, Deputy General Counsel for its parent corporation Travelers Group, Inc. and Executive Vice President and General Counsel for Gulf Insurance Group.

Mr. DeCarlo is a Certified ARIAS-US Arbitrator and Umpire, a Master Arbitrator for the NYS Insurance Department, and an Arbitrator for the American Arbitration Association and Center for Dispute Resolution. Mr. DeCarlo is also the Founder, Chairman and President of The American Society of Workers Comp Professionals, Inc. (AMCOMP). In addition, Mr. DeCarlo is a Director of 17 companies in the insurance industry.

Mr. DeCarlo has authored numerous scholarly articles in legal and trade journals and is a co-author of two books on workers compensation insurance, *Workers Compensation Insurance & Law Practice – The Next Generation* and *Stress in the American Workplace – Alternatives for the Working Wounded*. He Chairs an Advisory Committee of the World Trade Center Captive Insurance Company, and formerly served as Vice Chairman and Commissioner of the New York State Insurance Fund (NYSIF) for 10 years. He also served as an Inspector for the NYS Athletic Commission.

In communal life, Mr. DeCarlo is a Knight of Malta and a former Trustee of Mount St. Michael Academy. He recently received a Humanitarian Award for his efforts with the Judio-Christian tradition by the development Corporation of Israel. He has been honored by numerous major academic institutions such as Mount St. Michael and the College of Mount St. Vincent. He has also been honored by the Long Island Chapter of the Cystic Fibrosis Foundation and received AMCOMP'S certified Workers Compensation Professional (WCP) designation in 1999.

Mr. DeCarlo graduated from Iona College with a major in economics and earned his Law Degree at Saint John's University Law School. He and his wife MaryAnne, an artist, reside in Douglaston, NY.

Roger Thompson, WCP

Roger Thompson is a retiree from Travelers Insurance following thirty years of service in the area of Workers Compensation. Prior to his retirement, Mr. Thompson was Director for Worker's Compensation Legislative and Regulatory Issues. A graduate of the University of California, Santa Barbara, he began his career with Travelers in Des Moines, Iowa in 1969 and subsequently transferred to the Home Office in Hartford, Connecticut in 1976.

During his career with Travelers, Mr. Thompson worked with various trade associations including the American Insurance Association (AIA), The International Association of Industrial Accident Boards and Commissions (IAIABC) and served on the Research Committee at the Workers Compensation Research Institute (WCRI).

Mr. Thompson is married and the father of two sons and four grandchildren.

WORKERS COMPENSATION
The First One Hundred Years

TABLE OF CONTENTS

Introduction

Chapter One	Workers Compensation History and Workplace Safety	Page 1
Chapter Two	Employers and Employees Subject To the Workers Compensation Law	Page 7
Chapter Three	Security Arrangements and Underwriting	Page 13
Chapter Four	Standard Workers Compensation Policy, Endorsements and Federal Coverages	Page 19
Chapter Five	Covered Occupational Events	Page 25
Chapter Six	Mandated Benefits	Page 31
Chapter Seven	Cost Containment Strategies and Other Medical Issues	Page 37
Chapter Eight	Claims Handling, Fraud and Subrogation	Page 43
Chapter Nine	Program Administration	Page 49
Chapter Ten	The Rate-Making Process	Page 55
Chapter Eleven	Exclusive Remedy and Bad Faith	Page 61

WORKERS COMPENSATION
The First One Hundred Years
INTRODUCTION

This eleven-chapter course is designed to develop a basic foundation of knowledge of the various aspects of workers compensation so that individuals who have taken the course will have a better understanding and appreciation of how the various pieces of the workers compensation program (e.g. claims, risk management, pricing, etc.) work together in order to make the greater whole. Where appropriate, the material examines the pertinent approaches developed by the states since the first workmen's compensation laws were introduced in 1911.

The materials for this course have been developed from multiple sources and the text for the course is found in the book entitled *Workers Compensation: The First One Hundred Years*. This text was developed specifically for this course of study.

This course guide contains an introduction to each chapter, a chapter outline, and ten questions covering the material covered in the text book. These questions have been designed to cover the primary topics covered in each chapter.

The following serves to highlight the material covered in each of the eleven chapters:

> **Chapter One -** The early development of workmen's compensation laws (later to become workers compensation) in Europe is traced along with its subsequent development in the United States. With the passage of time, certain shortcomings of the program were recognized, and in 1972, a national commission was created to study the program and make recommendations for improvement. In response to these recommendations, states enacted substantial reforms in subsequent years. The chapter concludes with a discussion on the subject of workplace safety and the role of the Occupational Safety and Health Administration (OSHA) at the federal and state level.
>
> **Chapter Two –** The intended scope of workers compensation protection was universal coverage. Notwithstanding this intent, there are certain types of work activity (e.g., farm labors and domestics) that may, under certain circumstances, be difficult to cover. Additionally, many states originally had numeric exceptions to coverage along with other exceptions based on business type. The chapter examines the scope of workers compensation coverage along the issues associated with independent contractors, statutory employees and professional employee organizations (PEOs). The impact of

injuries occurring to out-of-state workers and to workers engaged in employment outside of their usual state of jurisdiction is also reviewed.

Chapter Three - Benefit security, and the various forms of that security, is examined in Chapter Three. Benefit security takes the form of insurance or individual or group self-insurance. Within the insurance mechanism, one finds private insurance, competitive or monopolistic state funds, and the residual market or assigned risk pools. While benefit security is a critical component of the program, responsible employers focus on workplace safety as the primary approach for purposes of reducing workplace injuries. The chapter concludes with an examination of the role of the underwriter along with the core elements associated with individual risk underwriting.

Chapter Four - Following an examination of the forms of benefit security covered in the previous chapter, this chapter shifts to an examination of the standard Workers Compensation and Employers Liability policy. Each section of the policy is reviewed with a copy of the policy available for purposes of perusal. The chapter includes a review of some of the more frequently used policy endorsements, along with an explanation of the particular situations in which the endorsements should be included with the policy. The chapter concludes with an examination of some of the various federal compensation programs involving the payment of benefits.

Chapter Five – The almost universal test for compensability of a workplace injury or death is that it must "arise out of and in the course of the employment." While the two phrases "arising out of" and "in the course of" the employment appear fairly straightforward in actual terminology, these phrases have been the subject of extensive litigation and expansion since their first enactment. A review of statutory provisions along with case law serves to depict how the subject has evolved over time and how it is being addressed legislatively in a number of jurisdictions. While many of the states originally a workplace injury to be a "personal injury by accident," with the of time, this restrictive term has evolved and today, the workers compensation program includes not only an expanded scope of covered injuries, but also a broad array of occupational diseases along with heart conditions and mental stress claims. Many of these conditions continue to be the subject of controversy and litigation today.

Chapter Six – The fundamental concept behind workers compensation is that the employer is responsible for certain benefits to an employee injured on the job without consideration for the issue of fault. These mandated benefits include the furnishing of medical care necessary for recovery and the payment of a portion of lost income in the instance of injury or death resulting from a work-related cause. This chapter examines the various types of benefits afforded through the workers compensation program along with the different forms of income replacement benefits that may be available to a worker who receives a work-related injury. Certain prescribed benefits are also payable to surviving dependents in the event of a work-related death.

Chapter Seven – The discussion of medical benefits available to injured workers under the workers compensation program is continued in this chapter with a focus on the factors influencing current medical cost increases. To address those increases, a number of cost containment strategies have been developed which include legislation regarding the choice of medical provider; the application of physician and hospital fee schedules; the development of treatment protocols; and the introduction of utilization review. This chapter delves into the subject of managed care at the state level and concludes with an examination of the issue of medical records privacy and *ex parte* communications.

Chapter Eight - Claims management and accident investigations are topics covered in this chapter. Claims management begins with a review of the role of the case manager along with the various functions associated case management. An important role for the claims adjuster is the timely and thorough conducting of an accident investigation. With the increasing cost associated with claims, there is also the rising concern for workers compensation fraud. Claims management also involves the recognition of subrogation potential and the way recoveries are handled in various jurisdictions.

Chapter Nine – This chapter reviews the claims administration process performed at the state level through a board, bureau, commission or other administrative state agency. Functions performed by these agencies include the promulgation of forms and regulations, the development of a dispute resolution process, along with functions designed to expedite and ensure the accuracy of benefit payments by insurers. The chapter concludes with an examination of the role of state second injury funds and special funds in terms of their original purposes(s) and the impact these funds have on overall program costs.

Chapter Ten - The method for determining workers' compensation rates – the manual rating system – and an examination of the subjects of experience rating and retrospective rating are covered in this chapter. The method of classification of risks is reviewed in some detail inasmuch as the classification system is the cornerstone of the rating process. Both experience rating and retrospective rating are programs available to employers of a certain size and are designed to make the cost for insurance more reflective of the employers actual experience.

Chapter Eleven - A central feature of the workers compensation program is the exclusive remedy doctrine. The *quid pro quo* of workers compensation calls for the employer to be responsible for wage replacement and the offering of necessary medical care in exchange for the injured employee foregoing any right to bring a direct action for damages against his/her employer. The limits of the exclusive remedy bargain are constantly being challenged and tested in the courts. Some of the more prevalent theories and situations under which these challenges are being brought today are identified in this chapter.

In addition to the above noted text, an AMCOMP Code Ethics has been developed that sets forth the minimum standards of individual conduct expected of those certified as Workers Compensation Professionals (WCP's). A copy of the AMCOMP Code of Ethics is included when ordering the course material.

The material covered in this eleven-chapter course is intended as a major building block in the creation of a foundation of a better understanding of workers compensation. The intent of the course of study is not to furnish a definitive answer on any of these topics, but rather to continue to put forth the best and freshest ideas that come to AMCOMP's® attention so that those who have taken the course of study will understand the many sides associated with each of these developing issues.

Upon completion of the first six chapters in the text and Course Guide, applicants seeking certification as a Workers Compensation Professional (WCP) are required to take a home study exam (based on the honor system). The exam is to be requested when the applicant has completed study of the first six chapters of the Course Guide. Following completion of the home study exam, the exam should be submitted for grading.

Upon completion of all eleven chapters, applicants are required to sit for a written, proctored exam. This exam is inclusive of all material covered in the text along with the AMCOMP® Code of Ethics. The exam will be administered in conjunction with AMCOMP® educational forums, seminars, and conferences, and other times arranged by AMCOMP®.

Successful completion of the exam will enable AMCOMP® to recognize an individual as a certified Workers Compensation Professional. Individuals will be issued a certification certificate and a WCP lapel pin. Ongoing educational opportunities will be available for WCP's at regular forums and educational seminars.

DISCLAIMER: The information contained in the course material is intended for informational purposes only and should not be construed as legal advice. The reader should seek competent legal counsel for advice on any legal matter.

CHAPTER ONE

WORKERS COMPENSATION HISTORY
AND
WORKPLACE SAFETY

Today in each state and the **District of Columbia**, workers compensation laws have been enacted to provide some degree of economic security to those who sustain an occupational injury or disease. These laws afford medical care and income replacement benefits following injury, illness or death that arises out of and in the course of employment.

Before the first workmen's compensation laws were enacted, a workers sole recourse for injury was under common law where, in order to obtain any recovery from the employer, the worker had to prove that the injury resulted from negligence on the part of the employer. In responding to such an action seeking damages, the employer could avail himself of certain defenses – contributory negligence, assumption of risk and the fellow-servant rule. Even in situations where injured workers were able to overcome those defenses, the court remedy proved to be slow, costly, and frequently uncertain.

Workmen's compensation had its genesis in Europe when German chancellor Otto Von Bismarck introduced the idea that Germany should provide for working people a system of insurance that would protect workers against the economic consequences resulting from sickness, accident or death. In 1884 Germany adopted the first modern workmen's compensation law, the Accident Insurance Law; thirteen years before England and twenty-five years before the first American jurisdiction enacted such a law.

At the close of the nineteenth century – as commercial enterprise expanded coincident with the Industrial Revolution – the number of workers injured or killed in this country increased as a result of work-related accidents. While the tort system struggled with the problem, states began to experiment with a benefit scheme that had its origin in Europe. **Maryland** passed the first workmen's compensation law in 1902, but it was limited in application and was ruled unconstitutional by the courts. Other early attempts to pass compensation laws suffered a similar fate, but states continued to pursue such action and in 1911, **Wisconsin** put in place the first compensation law still in effect today.

Early compensation laws had limitations in terms of who was covered, the level of benefits payable and the duration of entitlement. Over time, states have liberalized the benefit structure to ensure greater protection against the economic consequences of injury or death. A major stimulus to the expansion of benefits occurred in 1972 when the National Commission on State Workmen's Compensation Laws released their recommendations for an equitable compensation program. Consistent with recommendations made by the National

Commission, many state laws have been modified during the subsequent period so that they achieve a significant portion of the basic objectives set forth by the commission.

Responding to the recommendations of the National Commission, states expanded coverage of employers and employees and enhanced benefits available to replace income lost as a result of work-related disability and death. While the decades following the work of the National Commission resulted in improvements in multiple areas, new issues continue to confront the program. Today, rising health care costs, an aging population, along with rising costs for workers compensation coverage, all reflect problems that require addressing. The question of benefit adequacy continues to be the subject of debate among compensation experts.

Loss control and loss prevention require more than the commitment by the insurer and the offering of services. Workplace injuries are frequently the result of equipment failure, performance failure or education and training failure. Of these three, performance failures cause the most losses and are the most difficult to rectify. While corrective measures in education, training and equipment are easily identified and implemented, improved performance is dependent upon the attitudes of the employees and is thus more difficult to change.

Any discussion of workplace safety and loss prevention requires an examination of the role played by the Federal Occupational Safety and Health Act. Enacted in 1970, the Occupational Safety and Health Administration (OSHA) was established to *"Assure so far as possible every working man and woman in the nation safe and healthful working conditions."*

Coverage under OSHA is very extensive with few public employers being exempted from coverage. One of the more onerous responsibilities stemming from OSHA regulations is the reporting and record keeping requirements. Employers, with the exception of small employers, (ten employees or less) and employers in low-hazard industries (e.g., retail trade, finance, insurance, real estate and services) must record and report all workplace injuries and fatalities.

Nearly half of the states operate their own OSHA approved occupational safety and health program. These state programs are required to set up workplace safety and health standards at least as effective as comparable federal standards. States do have the option to promulgate standards covering hazards not covered by the federal standards.

Chapter One Outline

I. Workers Compensation History
   A. Social Responsibility Underlying Workers Compensation
   B. Recovery Under Common Law
      1. Contributory Negligence
      2. Fellow-Servant Rule
      3. Assumption of Risk
   C. Employers' Liability Laws
   D. Workmen's Compensation Laws in Europe
   E. Development of Workmen's Compensation in the United States
   F. The Formative Years
      1. Covered Workers
      2. Waiting Periods
      3. Medical Benefits
      4. Disability Benefits
      5. Death Benefits
   G. 1972 National Commission on State Workmen's Compensation Laws
      1. Nineteen Essential Recommendations
   H. Activity Following the Recommendations of the National Commission
      1. Activity in the 70s
      2. Activity in the 80s
      3. Activity in the 90s
      4. Opening Decades of the Twenty-First Century

II. Workplace Safety and Loss Prevention
   A. Developing an Effective Loss Control Program
   B. Federal Effort to Improve Workplace Safety and Health
      1. Occupational Safety and Health Administration (OSHA)
      2. National Institute for Occupational Safety and Health (NIOSH)
      3. Occupational Safety and Health Review Commission (OSHRC)
   C. OSHA Mission and Strategy
      1. Major Industrial Safety Regulations Promulgated By OSHA
   D. OSHA Penalties and Citations
   E. State OSHA Programs

Chapter One Exercises

(Practice exercises are sample questions of material covered within each chapter)

1. Describe the social philosophy behind workers compensation.

   Income replacement + med. benefits for victims of work related injuries

2. What was recovery under common law based upon and what were some of the problems associated with recovery under common law?

   - premise of fault

3. Describe the three defenses available to the employer under common law.

   (1) Contributory negligence - slightest act of ordinary care by worker barred them from recovery
   (2) Fellow-servant Rule (common employment) - notify employer if ee not doing job right/safe
   (3) Assumption of risk

4. How does recovery under a workers compensation law differ from recovery under common law?

   delay + uncertainty of enforcement, basis for damage amt. + ability to collect if you sued
   - prove wrong doing

5. What role did the 1972 National Commission play in improving state workers compensation programs?

   (1) provide broad cvg for ee work related injuries/disease
   (2) provide protection against lost wages
   (3) " " med. care + rehab
   (4) encourage safety
   (5) eff del. system

6. As the workers compensation program enters the twenty-first century, what are some of the important issues facing the program?

   (1) rising HC + Rx costs
   (2) Aging workforce
   (3) State movement → alt. benefit schemes

7. What type of violation might OSHA impose following a fatality occurring in the workplace? Serious or willful?

8. Identify some of the areas in which OSHA has promulgated safety regulations.

9. What was the purpose and scope of legislation signed in 1969 by President Nixon?
Coal mine health + safety Act for coal mining industry

10. How do the state OSHA programs interact with the federal program?

CHAPTER TWO

EMPLOYERS AND EMPLOYEES SUBJECT TO THE WORKERS COMPENSATION LAW

The principle of virtually universal coverage of all gainfully employed workers is a basic objective of the workers compensation program. With few exceptions employers and workers alike agree on the merit of this basic objective. For the employer, universal coverage represents a relatively inexpensive way to protect against the possibility of lawsuits that may result from a workplace injury or death. For the worker, coverage represents an important scheme of protection against the economic consequences that stem from a workplace injury.

Central to the issue of coverage is the question of what constitutes an employer-employee relationship. Unlike common law, most workers compensation laws require a contract of hire in order to establish an employment relationship. This contract may be expressed or implied, written or oral, but it should cover what is to be done, where and how it is to be done, and the remuneration that will be provided upon completion of the services.

In essence, the employment relationship is dependent upon who controls the progress of the work. Other factors that enter into the determination of the employment relationship include:

   (a) The right to hire and fire;
   (b) The method of payment for the services being provided;
   (c) Who is responsible for the furnishing of tools and the place of work; and
   (d) The "relative nature of the work"

While the concept of universal coverage has broad appeal, in point-of-fact, state laws do not cover all forms of work or occupations. It is estimated that the state workers compensation programs cover only about eighty percent of the wage and salary work force. For various political, economic or administrative reasons, state laws permit certain exceptions to coverage.

Most state laws make a specific exception for agricultural, domestic and casual workers. Casual employment is generally defined as one in which the employment is irregular, unpredictable, sporadic and brief. In addition, some jurisdictions require that the casual employment be outside of the normal business activities of the employer. Farm workers and domestic servants represent unique exposures that create difficulties in administering coverage. Other classes of employment create unique coverage issues.

In today's mobile economic environment, it is not uncommon for workers to travel between states and foreign countries. They may travel to attend business meetings or to conduct the employer's business in an adjoining state or distant jurisdiction. While the employer's workers compensation policy – especially for the smaller employer – is generally limited to the state where the employer has his/her principal business operation, the policy may not extend coverage to another state if the worker should be injured in some other state.

When a worker is principally employed in one state, and sustains a work-related injury in another state, that worker may have the option of claiming benefits under the law of the state where the injury occurred, depending on the law in the state of injury. The term "extraterritorial' as it applies to workers compensation has been defined as a *"Provision in workers compensation insurance under which an employee who incurs an injury in another state, and elects to come under the law of his/her home state, will retain coverage under the workers compensation coverage of his/her home state."* But the term can also be extended to include the worker who wants to come under the law of another state under certain circumstances.

A majority of states have addressed the subject of extraterritorial coverage. A number of states have enacted specific statutory provisions dealing with coverage for in-state workers who sustain an out-of-state injury, while a much larger number of states address both the issue of in-state coverage for workers who sustain an out-of-state injury and those out-of-state workers who sustain an in-state injury. Where the worker selects the benefits of the state of usual employment, there will generally not be a question of coverage. However, where the injured worker opts for the benefits payable in some other state, there may be a lack of insurance coverage if the employer has not included the other state when applying for insurance coverage.

It is common to recognize that the injured worker has the choice of selecting benefits from the state of principal employment or the state where the injury occurred. In addition to those two common scenarios, there are situations where injured workers have been entitled to seek benefits from the state where the original contract of employment was entered into. At the far extreme is the rare situation where the residence of the injured may be the determining factor as to what state's benefits are payable. Notwithstanding these potential options as to the state from which benefits are payable, state laws do not permit duplication of benefits. Where benefits are payable from one state, any other entitlement from another state is offset from the benefits payable from the first state.

In addition to the extraterritorial provisions found in the majority of states, a minority of states permit the employer and employee to enter into an express written agreement stipulating the benefits to be paid. This approach is not recognized in all states and case law has not always recognized the legality of such agreements. Similarly, states – particularly those states located in the Northwest – have entered into reciprocal agreements for purposes of determining what state is responsible for benefits in the case of an in-state injury.

Chapter Two Outline

I. Employers and Employees Subject to the Workers Compensation Law
    A. Coverage of Employees
        1. Numeric Exceptions
        2. Agricultural Laborers
        3. Casual Workers
        4. Domestics
        5. Family Members
        6. Sole Proprietors and Partners
        7. Executive Officers
        8. Illegal Aliens
        9. Real Estate Agents or Brokers
        10. Other Exempt Employees
    B. Independent Contractors
        1. Potential Advantages for the Employer
        2. Potential Disadvantages for the Employer
    C. Compensation Coverage and Independent Contractors
    D. Statutory Employees
    E. Professional Employer Organizations (PEOs)

II. Extraterritorial Coverage
    A. In-State Worker/Out-of-State Worker
    B. Out-of-State Worker/In-State Injury
    C. Express Written Agreements
    D. Reciprocal Agreements Between States

Chapter Two Exercises

(Practice exercises are sample questions of material covered within each chapter)

1. List some of the major components in determining whether an employment relationship exists?

2. What was the rationale for establishing numeric exceptions for coverage when the first workmen's compensation laws were enacted?

3. What might be some of the difficulties associated with providing workers compensation insurance for a sole proprietor?

4. What was the rationale for the early workmen's compensation laws excluding agricultural workers from coverage?

5. Are aliens who illegally entered this country eligible for workers compensation benefits if injured while at work?

6. What are some of the ways in which an employee is distinguished from an independent contractor?

7. When an employee is principally employed in one state and then conducts business or attends a meeting or conference in another state, what state may the employee seek benefits following a work-related injury?

8. What are some of the requirements that may apply in order for an out-of-state injury to be covered for an in-state employee?

9. Do the extraterritorial provisions in a state require that an injured worker accept the compensation benefits payable from that state?

10. Why are express written agreements generally considered ineffective in the majority of states to enlarge the applicability of that state's statute or to diminish the applicability of the statutes of other states?

CHAPTER THREE

SECURITY ARRANGEMENTS AND UNDERWRITING

There exist multiple sources from which employers subject to the workers compensation law can obtain coverage. In the four states of **North Dakota, Ohio, Washington** and **Wyoming**, insurance may be purchased through an exclusive state fund. In the remaining states and the **District of Columbia**, coverage may be purchased through private insurers licensed to conduct business in the state. Twenty-one states have legislatively created competitive state funds as an alternative to private insurance for purposes of affording coverage to employers seeking to insure.

Private insurers are permitted to write workers compensation coverage in all but the four monopolistic fund states. Where they are permitted to operate, they are subject to extensive state regulation. One of the key elements of insurance regulation is ensuring solvency. This is accomplished through regulator review of an insurer's valuation of liabilities and the nature and value of their assets.

For employers unable to purchase insurance or qualify as a self-insured, many states have established residual markets for the purpose of making available a market for obtaining insurance coverage. In certain states, the residual market is handled by the state competitive fund while in other states private insurers play a role in providing coverage.

An employer who provides compensation protection by means of demonstrating the financial ability to pay the compensation benefits required by law is known as a self-insurer. Employers may qualify to be responsible for their own risk – to be self-insured – in all states with the exception of **North Dakota** and **Wyoming**. Through a self-insurance program, the employer accepts primary financial and administrative responsibility for work-related injuries and deaths without the intervention of an insurance carrier. In a typical self-insurance program, the employer retains the first level of risk and may purchase excess insurance – a number of states require excess insurance or reinsurance as part of the self-insurance approval process.

While there may be variants in style, there are essentially two forms of self-insurance - individual self-insurance and group self-insurance. Individual self-insurance, as the name implies, means that a single employer has filed the required documentation and obtained approval from the particular jurisdiction(s) accepting the financial responsibility for any claims that might arise during the period of self-insurance. Presently, individual self-insurance is permitted in all jurisdictions with the exception of two monopolistic fund states – **North Dakota** and **Wyoming.**

Group self-insurance refers to the ability of a group of employers – the number and type of employers who may combine for purposes of self-insurance may vary by jurisdiction – who become jointly liable for the claims of members of the group. In consideration of a group self-insurance program, exposure to loss is not limited only to the individual employer, but takes on the responsibility for all members in the group.

One of the most critical tasks in ensuring the financial integrity of an insurance carrier is the proper underwriting of risks. The purpose of underwriting is to develop and maintain a profitable book of business. For underwriting to achieve that specified purpose, insurers must avoid adverse selection.

The underwriting process is essentially a decision-making endeavor. As such, underwriting follows the rules traditionally used in problem solving. The three basic steps to problem solving include: (1) gathering the body of information; (2) making a judgment about that information; and (3) acting on that judgment. In the case of workers compensation, underwriting guidelines can outline the information to be gathered; however, only experience combined with the application of common sense will provide the best basis for evaluating the risk under consideration and making a judgment regarding potential exposure.

Following the establishment of the appropriate classification of a risk, the workers compensation underwriter must also consider the work history of the employer and establish the attitude of management. The work history includes the length of time that the business has been in operation along with the physical hazard that the risk presents. There are certain general features that exist in varying degrees in every risk that have a marked effect on the potential for loss. These features stem from the employers approach to housekeeping, maintenance and hazard control.

Each of the features mentioned – housekeeping, maintenance and hazard control – contain numerous specific items for consideration. With the evolving workplace and changes in technology, these features require continual scrutiny to ensure that underwriting practices remain current with the current workplace. The quality of risk conditions on these points will alleviate or intensify all other risk hazards. Unfavorable conditions may actually create the potential for additional hazards.

Over time it has become apparent that a successful workers compensation insurance program requires active cooperation between the policyholder and the insurer. An important consideration is the willingness and ability of management to cooperate in efforts to minimize hazards and reduce losses. If the firm fails to have a safety program, or if the program is one that exists only on paper, it can generally be assumed that management has a passive attitude toward reducing workplace injuries.

Chapter Three Outline

I. Workers Compensation Security Arrangements
    A. Exclusive State Funds
    B. Competitive State Funds
    C. Private Insurance
    D. Residual Markets

II. Self-Insurance
    A. Individual Self-Insurance
        1. Specific Excess Coverage
        2. Aggregate Excess Coverage
    B. Self-Insurance Groups (SIG)
        1. Joint and Several Liability

III. Alternative Benefit Schemes

IV. Workers Compensation Underwriting
    A. Role of the Underwriter
    B. The Underwriting Process
    C. Core Elements of Individual Risk Underwriting
        1. Risk Classification
        2. Risk Conditions and Attitude
        3. Hazards and Their Control
        4. Housekeeping
        5. Maintenance
    D. Hazard Control
        1. Specific Hazards
        2. Catastrophic Hazards
        3. Hazard Information
    E. Loss History
    F. Risk pricing
    G. Other Underwriting Functions

Chapter Three Exercises

(Practice exercises are sample questions of material covered within each chapter)

1. Identify the primary forms of security arrangements that employers may use to satisfy their responsibility under the law.

2. Explain the difference between a competitive state fund and a monopolistic state fund.

3. What are the two different types of private insurers?

4. What are the principal liabilities carried on an insurer's balance sheet?

5. Describe the purpose and scope of the residual market.

6. What is meant by the term "joint and several liability" in a self-insurance program?

7. List and describe the three core elements of individual risk underwriting?

8. List four of the seven specific items described in the text that should be examined when evaluating the issue of housekeeping for a potential account.

9. List four specific areas that an underwriter should consider when evaluating the issue of maintenance for a potential account.

10. Identify the aspects of management attitude that need to be considered by the underwriter and describe how that attitude might influence loss exposure.

CHAPTER FOUR

THE STANDARD WORKERS COMPENSATION POLICY, ENDORSEMENTS AND FEDERAL COVERAGES

The current Workers Compensation and Employers Liability Policy is referred to as the "Standard Policy" because insurance carriers are required to use the prescribed policy language. The workers compensation policy is designed to accomplish two purposes. The first purpose is to pay the statutory benefits specified by the compensation law of those states listed on the Information Page. The second purpose is to cover the liability arising from a workplace injury when legal action is brought seeking damages other than the benefits provided under the compensation law.

Review of the standard policy will provide the reader with the language used by virtually every insurance company. The current policy consists of a General Section and six parts - each part is self-contained. Briefly, the General Section and the associated parts cover the following topics:

General Section - establishes that the policy is a contract of insurance between the employer identified in the Information Page and the insurer.

Part One: **Workers Compensation Insurance** - sets forth the company's agreement to provide benefits required of the insured by the workers compensation law of the states identified on the Information Page.

Part Two: **Employers Liability Insurance** - establishes the company's agreement to pay all sums – subject to policy limits - on account of the legal liability of the employer for damages because of bodily injury to an employee. Certain exclusions pertain to the coverage available under Part Two.

Part Three: Other States Insurance - provides that coverage applies if the employer begins work in any state designated in Item 3.C. of the Information Page along with the requirement on the part of the employer to notify the insurer if the employer begins operation in a state not listed on the Information Page.

Part Four: Your Duties if Injury Occurs – sets forth the duties and responsibilities of the employer following the occurrence of an injury.

Part Five: Premium - provisions relative to the development of premiums are described. Records needed to compute premium are to be maintained and turned over to the insurer.

Part Six: Conditions - conditions applicable to the operation of the Policy are set forth in this final policy part.

The Information Page – formerly referred to as the Declaration Page – details the important components of the insurance contract between the employer and the insurer. The Information Page includes the name of the insured; the period covered by the policy; limits of coverage under the policy along with a listing of the states covered; and a demonstration of the estimated annual premium.

In addition to the coverage afforded through the standard Workers Compensation and Employers Liability Policy, endorsements have been developed for purposes of expanding coverage, excluding coverage, and simplifying administration. Endorsements are written agreements attached to a policy that have been adopted by the industry rate-making organization or by the independent state rating organizations in the remaining states. Prior to being used in a particular jurisdiction, endorsements must be approved by the state insurance regulator. Policy endorsements may serve to modify the coverage provided under the law of various states, or may operate to extend coverage to include federal exposures.

Beyond the scope of policy endorsements lies the Certificate of Insurance. The certificate serves to demonstrate to external interests the existence of an insurance Policy along with a description of the location and operations covered. While demonstrative of the existence of an insurance policy, the certificate itself does not serve to provide insurance.

In addition to the large number of general and individual state endorsements, there are a number of federal compensation programs designed to address coverage for certain federal exposures. These include:

- Federal Employers' Compensation Act (FECA)
- Federal Employers Liability Act (FELA)
- Federal Coal Mine and Safety Act (CMHSA)
- Radiation Exposure Compensation Act (RECA)
- Energy Employees Occupational Illness Compensation Program Act (EEOICPA)
- Death on the High Seas Act
- Merchant Marine Act (Jones Act)

Because of a United States Supreme Court holding that state workers compensation laws did not apply on the nation's navigable waters, the Longshore and Harbor Workers Compensation Act (LHWCA) was enacted to cover injuries that occur during maritime employment on "navigable waters" of the United States. Through a series of amendments, coverage was extended to include several miscellaneous classes of employees through the following extensions to the law:

- Defense Base Act Coverage Endorsement
- Federal Coal Mine Health and Safety Act Coverage Endorsement
- Non-appropriated Instrumentalities Act Coverage Endorsement

Chapter Four Outline

I. The Standard Workers Compensation Policy
    A. General Section
    B. Part One – Workers Compensation Insurance
    C. Part Two – Employers Liability Insurance
    D. Part Three – Other States Insurance
    E. Part Four – Your Duties If Injury Occurs
    F. Part Five – Premium
    G. Part Six – Conditions
    H. Information Page
    I. Binders, Renewals and Cancellations

II. Workers Compensation Policy Endorsements

III. Federal Compensation Programs
    A. Federal Employees Compensation Act (FECA)
    B. Federal Employers Liability Act (FELA)
    C. Federal Coal Mine Health and Safety Act (CMHSA)
    D. Radiation Exposure Compensation Act (RECA)
    E. Energy Employees Occupational Illness Compensation Program Act (EEOICPA)
    F. Death on the High Seas Act
    G. Merchant Marine Act of 1920 (Jones Act)
    H. Longshore and Harbor Workers Compensation Act (LHWCA)
        1. Defense Base Act
        2. Nonappropriated Fund Instrumentalities Act
        3. Outer Continental Shelf Lands Act

Chapter Four Exercises

(Practice exercises are sample questions of material covered within each chapter)

1. What type of claims will not be defended under Part One of the policy?

2. How do the policy coverage limits under Part Two of the policy differ from those contained in Part One of the policy?

3. When does the duty to defend a claim under Part Two of the policy cease?

4. Is coverage available under Part Two of the policy for activities such as defamation of character, sexual harassment, humiliation or discrimination? If they are not covered, why?

5. What must the employer do if that employer establishes a business operation in another state?

6. How is an employer's final premium determined?

7. What purposes are served by the use of a workers compensation policy endorsement?

8. What provisions found in a state workers compensation law may prompt the need for use of the Voluntary Compensation Endorsement?

9. The Voluntary Compensation and Employers Liability Coverage Endorsement protects those workers not otherwise subject to the workers compensation law. What conditions must such an employee follow in order to obtain benefits under the endorsement?

10. How does recovery under the "Jones Act" or the Federal Employers Liability Act (FELA) differ from recovery under the Longshore and Harbor Workers Compensation Act (LHWCA)?

CHAPTER FIVE

COVERED OCCUPATIONAL EVENTS

The almost universal test for compensability of a workplace injury or death is that it must "arise out of "and" in the course of the employment." The "arising out of" portion of the phrase is intended to mean that the injury must be work-related to the extent that there is a direct causal connection between the injury and the employment. In determining the causal relationship between an injury and the employment, the "arising out of" concept is concerned with the type of risk to which a worker is exposed by reason of the employment.

A number of jurisdictions adhere to the "actual risk" doctrine where it is required only that the employment subjects the worker to the actual risk that results in injury. This represents a deviation from the "positional risk" doctrine which infers that an injury arises out of the employment if it would not have occurred *but for* the fact that the employment obligation placed the worker in a position where the injury occurred.

Injuries resulting from personal conditions of the worker are in most instances found to "arise out of the employment" where the employment contributed to the final disability by placing the employee in a position where the condition was aggravated or accelerated by the workplace strain or trauma. Back and health conditions that pre-dated the actual occurrence of a workplace injury are examples of these types of personal conditions.

Determination of what constitutes the "course of employment" is likewise frequently the subject of controversy and litigation. Using a literal interpretation of the wording, compensation would be payable only for those injuries sustained during working hours on the premises of the employer while engaged in activities that were unquestionably work-related. Following such an approach would result in fewer work place injuries qualifying for benefits and would be contrary to the basic intent behind workers compensation. Statements concerning whether the "course of employment" test has been met vary with the categories of employment relationships. An injury occurring in the same factual situation may result in either an award or denial of compensation benefits, depending upon the relationship that exists.

Many states modeled their original workmen's compensation laws after the English Workmen's Compensation Act of 1897, which included reference to "personal injury by accident." The intent of this language was to ensure that employers were only responsible for unintended injuries stemming from a clearly identifiable workplace incident. For many years a work-related injury in many states had to have been caused by a single, discrete incident in order to be found compensable. A basic element of the term "accidental" implies that at least some part of the incident must be unexpected.

In most instances today, it is held that the "accident" requirement is met where either the cause of the injury was unanticipated or the injury itself was the unexpected result of the normal performance of a duty or task. In the majority of jurisdictions, an injury will be treated as accidental if the usual work or exertion results in strain or breakage. Similarly, the majority of jurisdictions hold the "by accident" requirement to include injuries resulting from usual work exertion and other situations that may be less well-defined than traumatic injuries.

The term "injury" is defined in some states as "damage or harm to the physical structure of the body and such diseases or infections as naturally result therefrom." Following modern concepts of disability, courts have generally construed various non-traumatic events as cumulative or gradual injury as covered under the compensation law. Thus, courts have awarded compensation for conditions that stemmed from repetitive injurious exposures over a period of a few days to several decades.

In the case of occupational disease, establishing a connection to the workplace exposure is frequently difficult to demonstrate. Because of this difficulty, states were slow in terms of extending coverage to diseases that arose out of the employment. In large part, the difficulties associated with occupational disease result from the interrelated issues of the long latency period for many occupational diseases and establishing medical causation. Establishing medical causation in an occupational disease claim involves three essential components. The first is whether there is a sufficiently established causal link between an occupational exposure and a particular disease. The second addresses the question as to whether the claimant actually has the disorder being claimed. The third and final component is whether the alleged occupational exposure caused the disease.

Similar to the situation with respect to back injuries, claims involving heart attacks, strokes and other cardiac conditions are some of the more troublesome problems facing the workers compensation program. The difficulty in determining compensability of heart attacks and other cardiac conditions stems from (1) the lack of a direct link between the heart condition and the victim's employment; (2) there may be pre-existing conditions; and (3) the fact that current medical technology is not able to establish what may combine to produce a heart attack.

Like heart conditions, mental health problems may be related to a multitude of conditions (e.g., stress, depression, work pressure) and for the workers compensation program, the challenge is to separate out the possible influence of the family, the community, and other social influences/actors from the work environment. To provide some means for differentiating between the various forms that mental claims may take, three categories of mental claims have been identified. These include physical-mental claims, mental-physical claims, and mental–mental claims. While the first two categories are recognized as compensable in the majority of states, it is the third category – mental-mental claims - that prompt the most litigation for the workers compensation program.

Chapter Five Outline

I. "Arising Out of" the Employment
    A. Risk Doctrines
        1. Peculiar or Increased Risk Doctrine
        2. Actual Risk
        3. Positional Risk
    B. Assault
    C. Horseplay
    D. Acts of God
    E. Suicide
    F. War and Terrorism

II. "In the Course of" Employment
    A. Employee Misconduct
    B. "Going and Coming" Rule
    C. Personal Comfort Doctrine
    D. Traveling Employees
    E. Telecommuting
    F. Recreational, Social and Athletic Activities

III. Compensability Standards
    A. Types of Injuries Covered
        1. Personal Injury by Accident
        2. Accidental Injury
        3. Personal Injury
    B. Presumption of Injury
    C. Gradual or Cumulative Injury
    D. Pre-existing Risk and Injury Aggravation
    E. Occupational Disease
    F. Occupational Disease Provisions
    G. Presumption in the Case of Occupational Disease
    H. Heart Conditions
    I. Mental Stress Claims
        1. Physical-Mental
        2. Mental-Physical
        3. Mental-Mental

Chapter Five Exercises

(Practice exercises are sample questions of material covered within each Chapter)

1. What is the two-fold test for determining the compensability of work place injuries or death in most states?

2. Describe the various tests that have been developed by the courts for the purpose of determining whether a workplace injury or death "arose out of the employment."

3. What type of workplace injury is covered by the "positional risk" doctrine?

4. What type of events might be referred to as "Acts of God?"

5. Describe the factors that are considered when making a determination as to whether a workplace injury or death arose "in the course of the employment."

6. What are some of the difficulties associated with determining whether an injury occurring to an employee "working at home" is covered under the workers compensation law?

7. Describe the difference between a workplace injury that results from an assault and one that is the result of horseplay.

8. How has the workers compensation system moved over time to include more claims under the term "accidental injury?"

9. What difficulties are confronted in attempting to hold a heart attack claim as compensable?

10. What are the three categories of mental injury claims? Give a brief example of each type of claim

CHAPTER SIX

MANDATED BENEFITS

The fundamental concept behind workers compensation is that the employer is responsible for certain benefits to an employee injured on the job, without consideration for the issue of fault. The benefits to which an injured employee may be entitled include access to the medical care or treatment required to effect complete recovery and the replacement of a portion of lost wages during the period of recovery, or, in the case of death, during a period of dependency.

Medical benefits encompass the furnishing of necessary care and treatment to achieve maximum medical recovery. Medical coverage is provided from the first dollar without limit as to duration or dollar amount. In addition, medical benefits continue for the duration of the period of recovery and are thereby not subject to any maximum duration or payable amount. For the most part, the same basic benefits are covered in every state. Generally, covered medical benefits include podiatric, osteopathic, chiropractic, surgical, hospital, prescription drugs and dental care though limits may be imposed on the maximum utilization of some of these services. Psychotherapy and other psychiatric treatment may be included if regarded as necessary for the injured worker's recovery. Chiropractic or podiatric treatments, supplies such as wheelchairs or wrist braces, orthopedic mattresses, and nursing services may also be specifically authorized.

Physical and vocational rehabilitation benefits are available to workers following a work-related injury. Rehabilitation is intended to (1) eliminate the disability completely; (2) reduce or alleviate the disability to the greatest degree possible; or (3) retrain the injured worker to live and function within the limits of the disability but to the maximum of his or her capabilities.

Income replacement benefits for an injured worker are generally based upon a portion of the weekly earnings – generally two-thirds of the worker's prior weekly earnings – subject to a maximum and minimum weekly compensation benefit rate set by the state. Benefits for income replacement begin following a waiting period set forth in the statute. Where time away from work continues beyond a prescribed number of days, again set by statute, the worker is compensated for the time period covered by the original waiting period.

There are a number of specific forms of income replacement or disability benefits. These include:

- Temporary Total Disability (TTD) – Benefit payable where the inability to work as a result of a work-related injury exceeds the statutory waiting period.

- Temporary Partial Disability (TPD) – Where the injured worker is earning less or is working fewer hours as a result of a workplace injury, benefits are available to replace a portion of the earnings lost.

- Permanent Total Disability (PTD) - Benefit payable where the workplace injury or disease incapacitates the worker to the extent that he or she will no longer be able to engage in any form of gainful employment.

- Permanent Partial Disability (PPD) – Benefits payable for the real or projected loss of future earnings resulting from a workplace injury. Benefits for PPD may be either scheduled or unscheduled awards.

In those states where scheduled PPD awards are payable, such benefits are payable in accordance with a list of body parts (e.g., arm, leg, foot, hand, etc.) where a set number of weeks (the schedule) of compensation benefits are payable for the complete loss or loss of use of the body member. Where loss or loss of use is less than total, the maximum number of weeks is reduced in proportion to the percentage of the loss or loss of use.

Unscheduled PPD awards generally focus on injuries to the back, psychiatric ailments, heart and vascular ailments, and other conditions not found within the schedule. A number of theories of entitlement have evolved relative to the appropriate method for compensating for PPD. Some theories focus solely on the economic consequences resulting from the injury, while other approaches strive to compensate for the reduction in functional ability or the impact on the quality of life. There are four recognized methods for compensating unscheduled awards.

- Impairment Based

- Loss-of-Wage-Earning-Capacity

- Wage-Loss

- Bi-furcated Approach

In the case of a work-related death, survivor's benefits are payable to the surviving spouse and/or dependent children upon the death of the worker. In the majority of states, death benefits are payable at the same rate as the benefit for total disability. In addition to the periodic benefits, a burial allowance is also payable following a work-related death.

Chapter Six Outline

I. Workers Compensation Mandated Benefit
    A. Medical and Hospital Benefits
    B. Covered Medical Expenses
        1. Prescription Drugs
        2. Artificial Members
        3. Attendant Care
    C. Independent Medical Examinations (IMEs)
    D. Vocational and Physical Rehabilitation
        1. Purpose of Vocational and Physical Rehabilitation
        2. Workers Compensation Benefits During Rehabilitation
    E. Income Replacement Benefits
        1. Jurisdictional Waiting and Retroactive Periods
        2. Statutory Maximum and Minimum Compensation Benefits
        3. Disability Benefit Duration
    F. Disability Benefit Computation
    G. Types Of Disability Benefits
        1. Temporary Total Disability (TTD)
        2. Permanent Total Disability (PTD)
        3. Temporary Partial Disability (TPD)
        4. Permanent Partial Disability (PPD)
            a. Schedules Awards
            b. Unscheduled Awards
                i. Impairment-Based Benefits
                ii. Loss of Wage Earning Capacity (LWEC)
                iii. Wage Loss
                iv. Bi-furcated Approach
    H. Disfigurement Benefits
    I. Survivor Benefits
    J. Benefit Escalation and Offset Provisions
    K. Safety Violations

Chapter Six Exercises

(Practice exercises are sample questions of material covered in each chapter)

1. What medical expenses are covered in a compensable workers compensation claim?

2. What are the three primary objectives of physical or vocational rehabilitation?

3. Most states establish the weekly disability benefit as a percentage of the workers average weekly wage. Five states base benefits on the workers "spendable income." How is spendable income defined?

4. Identify and describe briefly the four different types of disability benefits.

5. What is the generic form of the statutory definition for permanent total disability?

6. What is a scheduled permanent partial disability benefit?

7. Describe the three basic theories underlying compensation for an unscheduled permanent partial disability.

8. What other factors may be taken into consideration when compensation benefits are awarded on the basis of "loss of earning capacity."

9. In the case of a work-related death, who is generally presumed to be a dependent?

10. What are the purposes served by benefits escalation and the enactment of "reverse offset" provisions?

CHAPTER SEVEN

COST CONTAINMENT STRATEGIES AND

OTHER MEDICAL ISSUES

As described previously, medical benefits encompass the furnishing of necessary care and treatment to affect maximum medical recovery. Medical coverage is provided from the first dollar and is not subject to any deductible or co-payment arrangements. Medical includes the services of a medical provider, care rendered at a medical facility – either in-patient or outpatient – and any drugs or prescriptions prescribed by a treating physician, without limit as to duration or dollar amount.

Benefits for rehabilitation take the form of either physical rehabilitation or vocational rehabilitation. Physical rehabilitation encompasses those services required to reduce or alleviate the extent of the disability to the degree possible. Vocational rehabilitation is concerned with providing the injured worker with retraining or the development of job skills necessary to return the employee as a productive member of the community.

The cornerstone of effective claims management is the ability to understand and effectively interact with physicians and other health care professionals relative to medical issues. With increases in the amount expended for medical in a workers compensation claim, the medical portion of the benefit dollar is approaching two-thirds in many jurisdictions. With further increases in medical cost inflation anticipated for the foreseeable future, this proportion is expected to continue to increase.

The question of what constitutes adequate, prompt, and appropriate medical care may differ with the type of injury involved. Most workplace injuries are relatively minor – approximately three-fourths of all injuries do not result in disability sufficient to fulfill waiting period requirements for income replacement benefits. The most common injuries are strains and sprains, bruises, contusions, abrasions, and cuts and lacerations. These types of injuries are generally treated immediately and leave no permanent residuals.

For the less common but more serious occupational injury or disease, the medical treatment may be long and complex. Emergency room care may not be enough; medical rehabilitation may be necessary. For a small percentage of all workplace injuries there may be some permanent residual effect. Where the permanent residual effect is serious, both medical and vocational rehabilitation may be necessary.

Today, much of what is found in the workers compensation medical arena can be classified under the general category of managed care. While managed care encompasses a great many claims practices, its genesis was with coverage available for general health conditions.

However, this chapter will provide a general overview of the concept of managed care as it has been applied in workers compensation. The following lists the more prominent components of managed care:

- **Selection or choice of the treating physician** – Many states give the employer the right to select or choose the treating provider. In other states, the injured worker has the right of selection, or may be limited to selecting the treating physician from a panel or list of providers.

- **Medical fee schedules** – A growing number of states have administratively introduced medical fee schedules for purposes of setting the maximum rates payable for certain medical procedures.

- **Utilization review and medical bill review** – Utilization review (UR) may occur prospectively (before the treatment is rendered), concurrently (at the time the treatment is being provided), or retrospectively (following the providing of the medical services). Medical bill review, while looking only at the fees charged for services, is designed to ensure that billing practices and reimbursements are consistent with the medical fee schedule, or with "usual and customary" charges where a medical fee schedule does not exist.

- **Independent medical examinations (IMEs)** – Regulations promulgated by individual states determine when the IME may be conducted, who is an appropriate physician to conduct the IME, and at what intervals an IME may be requested.

- **Return-to-work and transitional work programs** – The objective of all parties following the occurrence of a workplace injury should be directed at timely return to work. Efforts to this end may involve simply work schedule changes or may require the transition to a completely new job or occupation.

A developing concern among a growing number of Americans is the question as to who is entitled to have access to medical care records, and how that health care information may be used. The Federal government, through the enactment of and promulgation of regulations under the Health Insurance Portability and Accountability Act (HIPAA), has sought to address those concerns. All handlers of such information have a duty and responsibility to ensure that such information is subject to proper usage.

Chapter Seven Outline

I. Medical Coverage and Cost Containment Strategies
    A. Factors Prompting Medical Cost Increases
        1. Cost Shifting
        2. Prescription Drugs
        3. Technology
        4. Litigation
    B. Cost Containment Strategies
        1. Choice of Medical Provider
        2. Medical Fee Schedules
            a. Fees for Medical Services
            b. Fees for Hospital Services
            c. Prescription Monitoring Program (PMP)

II. Managed Care
    A. Managed Care Networks
        1. Health Maintenance Organizations
        2. Preferred Provider Organizations
        3. Point-of-Service
    B. Workers Compensation Managed Care Networks
    C. Components of Managed Care Arrangements
        1. Medical Bill Review and Bill Repricing
        2. Utilization Review
        3. Treatment Guidelines
        4. Medical Case Management

III. Medicare Set-Aside Arrangements

IV. Medical Records Privacy
    A. Federal Medical Privacy Requirements

V. The Affordable Care Act (ACA)

Chapter Seven Exercises

(Practice exercises are sample questions of material covered within each chapter)

1. What are the unique features of medical coverage under the workers compensation program that distinguish it from other forms of health care coverage?

2. What are the three arguments that serve to favor the employee's choice of medical provider?

3. What purposes are served by the states introduction of a workers compensation medical fee schedule?

4. What type of medical services may be covered under a workers compensation medical fee schedule?

5. What is workers compensation managed care?

6. What are the three objectives of managed care?

7. What does utilization review in a managed care arrangement consist of?

8. What are "conditional payments" made under the Medicare program?

9. Under Health and Human Services (HHS) regulations, what rights does the consumer have relative to his/her own medical information?

10. What do some observers speculate as to the potential impact of the Affordable Care Act on workers compensation claims?

CHAPTER EIGHT

CLAIMS HANDLING, FRAUD AND SUBROGATION

Workers compensation claims management is composed of many processes including the establishment of the claim, claims investigation, assessment of liability, and medical and litigation management to name but a few of the more predominant. Many of the processes are in a state of change resulting from advances in technology along with the identification of new and more effective management approaches.

The case manager plays a critical role in the claims process. In most instances, the case manager is responsible for reviewing the First Report of Injury (FROI), setting up the claim file, determining whether the claim requires some form of investigation, and the ongoing activities including the timely closure of the claim. Included within the functions of the case manager is the filing of the FROI with the appropriate state administrative agency so as to notify the agency of the occurrence of an injury so that the monitoring of the benefits can begin.

Where a claims investigation or case follow-up is necessary, the claim is directed to a claims adjuster. The adjuster tends to be the focal point of contact with the injured worker, the employer, the medical provider or other individuals associated with the claim. To accomplish these activities, the adjuster must have good communication skills, must be a good listener, and possess a basic understanding of human nature and motivation principles.

The general code of conduct for insurance adjusters adopted in 1939 prohibits adjusters from dealing directly with claimants known to have legal representation or from dispensing legal advice. Under the code of conduct, adjusters are also required to identify any conflicts of interest to policyholders and to provide copies of transcripts or statements to any party interviewed.

Claims investigations take different paths depending upon the circumstances surrounding the alleged injury. Where the claim involves a fatality or where there is likely to be a question of compensability or action against a third party, it is generally advisable to conduct an in-person interview. Whether the investigation is conducted in-person or via a telephone interview, it is important that it be done in a timely fashion. The passage of time serves to obscure the memory and the facts surrounding the injury.

One of the responsibilities of the claims adjuster in conducting an investigation is to identify any potential fraud. Since the cost crisis of workers compensation that began to arise in the 1980s, a recurring theme has been the extent of fraud in workers compensation. While allegations of fraud are not confined to the arena of benefits payable to employees, warning signs or indications of the potential for fraud have been developed. As the accident investigation unfolds, the adjuster needs to be aware of these signs for purposes of addressing the potential for fraud at the outset of a claim.

In addition to the potential for fraud stemming from the alleged injury, there is also the potential of fraud arising during the course of treatment being provided by the treating physician, or by the attorney or legal representative of the employee. The adjuster must be diligent in all respects of the claim to ensure that appropriate benefits are being paid and that all efforts are being directed toward the timely return-to-work.

Workers compensation fraud is not confined solely to those situations involving injured workers or the treatment or legal advice they are receiving. Insurers must also be aware of the potential for fraud extending from the employer in the determination of risk classifications and the amount of payroll that is part of the premium calculation. Employers, sometimes alone and sometimes in conjunction with unscrupulous agents or brokers, have derived means to circumvent appropriate premium charges. It must be remembered that workers compensation fraud, whether part of a claim or part of coverage, is a serious offense and results in higher premiums and higher costs for products and services.

A further role of the adjuster when conducting an investigation is to identify any potential subrogation recovery. The principle of subrogation dictates that an insurer who has paid a loss under an insurance policy is entitled to all the rights and remedies belonging to the insured against a third party with respect to any loss covered by the policy. Essentially, subrogation allows an insurer who has indemnified an insured to stand in the shoes of the insured in regards to the insured's claim for compensation against a third party.

When addressing the subject of subrogation in any line of insurance – including workers compensation – it is important to keep in mind the issue of contributory negligence. While contributory negligence is not a factor when considering the payment of workers compensation benefits, contributory negligence, depending upon the state or jurisdiction, is an issue of major consideration when an injured worker is seeking damages from a negligent third party.

When dealing with a waiver of subrogation, it is important to recognize that any such waiver does not prevent the injured worker from bringing a direct action for damages against a third party responsible for the worker's injury. The waiver of subrogation only precludes the injured worker's employer and workers compensation insurer or benefit administrator from initiating a subrogation action and/or from enforcing its lien on a third-party claim. The insurer may proceed with recovery of any payments the insurer has made from the injured worker's recovery.

Chapter Eight Outline

I. Case Manager Role
    A. Coverage Verification
    B. Establishment of the Claim File
    C. Benefit Initiation and Monitoring
    D. Case Reserving
        1. Medical
        2. Indemnity
        3. Expenses
    E. Information Compilation and Data Collection
    F. Timely Closure of Claims

II. Accident Investigation
    A. Code of Conduct for Adjusters
    B. Conducting an Investigation

III. Attorney-Client Privilege and Work-Product Doctrine

IV. Fraud
    A. Fraud versus Abuse
    B. Perpetrators of Workers Compensation Fraud
        1. Fraud Perpetrated by Workers
            a. Self-inflicted or intentional Injury
            b. The "Monday" morning injury
            c. Malingering or working while allegedly disabled
        2. Employer Fraud
            a. Under reporting of payroll
            b. Misclassification of payroll
        3. Medical Provider Fraud
        4. Attorney Fraud
        5. Insurer Fraud
    C. Fraud Prevention

V. Subrogation
    A. Aspects Associated with Subrogation Recovery
        1. Time Frame for Seeking Recovery
        2. Allocation of Expenses
        3. Distribution of Recovery
        4. Excess Recovery Distribution
    B. Comparative and Contributory Negligence
    C. Negligence on the Part of the Employer
    D. Waiver of Subrogation

Chapter Eight Exercises

(Practice exercises are sample questions of material covered within each chapter)

1. What are the initial steps to be taken by the employer following awareness of a workplace injury?

2. What activities undertaken by the case manager following the reporting of a claim are oftentimes viewed as administrative tasks?

3. List several of the claim situations that almost always warrant a formal investigation.

4. The attorney-client privilege ensures that communication between the client and the attorney may not be revealed to other persons. What elements must take place in order for the privilege to exist?

5. What are the three elements of the work-product doctrine?

6. What is the difference between workers' compensation fraud and abuse?

7. Describe some of the specific areas where workers compensation fraud may occur.

8. Identify and briefly describe at least five of the warning signs of potential employee fraud.

9. What purposes are served by subrogation?

10. Does the waiver of subrogation prevent the injured worker from bringing a direct action for damages against a third party responsible for the worker's injury?

CHAPTER NINE

PROGRAM ADMINISTRATION

Administration of the workers compensation law and the awarding of compensation benefits areis under the jurisdiction of a workers compensation board, commission or similar state administrative agency. In virtually every state, the administrative agency operates under the supervision or direction of the state's Department of Labor or equivalent. The state administrative agency is entrusted with the responsibility to enforce the law ensuring coverage of employers, receive claims, monitor the delivery of benefits, make decisions and awards, and conduct informal and formal hearings to resolve disputes.

The claims process begins with the filing of a notice of loss. The filing of the injury notice is sufficient in the majority of instances to prompt the payment of compensation benefits due. Where there is a question or dispute relative to entitlement, there is a time limit for filing a formal claim for benefits. The time limit for filing such a claim is generally two years following the date of the accident or in the case of an occupational disease, two years from the manifestation of the condition and knowledge of its relationship to the employment.

Proper monitoring of claim activity by the administrative agency requires timely access to information. Until the 1980s, states relied upon the employer and/or insurer to submit information to the agency on paper forms. Outside of some basic information included with the FROI states varied widely in terms of the level of detail they required. With advances in the area of technology, an effort was undertaken to standardize the information being reported and to expedite the transfer of information through electronic data interchange (EDI).

Beginning in 1991, members of the International Association of Industrial Accident Boards and Commissions (IAIABC) undertook an effort to standardize the data collection process and look for ways to efficiently collect the information. The listing of recommended data elements was compiled over a period of time during which insurance regulators, state program administrators, insurance carriers, and self-insured employers, identified those articles of information that would develop a core of data elements in order to provide credible management and financial information.

Once the means are established for the collection of data, there must be a purpose for the collection of the data. System administrators, concerned with identifying ways to improve program performance, agreed to develop program benchmarks in order to measure performance among jurisdictions. Expansion of the data collection process along with the approaches to benchmarking continue to be a ongoing project at the IAIABC.

Injured workers have the right to be represented by an attorney. State laws do vary in terms of the method in which attorney fees will be awarded. In most states the attorney fee comes out of any award. Most states establish the actual allowable amount of attorneys' fees by statute or regulation. Frequently organizations such as trade unions have licensed claimants' representatives who assist members in the connection with the filing of claims and any representation at hearings.

For claims that involve some level of controversy, states have created a wide spectrum of methods - including informal and formal dispute resolution forums, as well as appellate forums – to resolve these differences. The last ten years have seen many states make more of an effort to resolve disputes through informal means. At present, fully four-fifths of all jurisdictions hold pre-hearing conferences before conducting a formal hearing. The most common pattern for the resolution of disputes is some form of informal process, followed by a formal hearing with the opportunity for administrative appellate review. All jurisdictions permit appeals from the appellate review to the civil courts.

A subject of growing interest for many states has been the continuing role and purpose of the state second injury funds. Second injury funds were created as a means to encourage employers to hire and retain workers with pre-existing physical disabilities. Because a pre-existing condition might increase the disability should a second injury occur, employers were reluctant to hire or retain workers with disabilities. Second injury funds were designed to afford some economic relief to employers where a subsequent injury occurred to a person with a previous disability.

In light of certain other federal legislation that operates to encourage employers to hire those with disabilities, along with growing concern for the states' unfunded liabilities, a growing number of states have recently repealed their second injury fund laws for newly arising claims. Currently sixteen states have enacted laws repealing their second injury fund and a number of additional states are studying the issue.

Special funds serve a multitude of purposes. Beyond the scope of compensating in the instance of second injuries, a number of special funds have been established for the purpose of either paying directly or reimbursing the employer/insurer for supplemental benefits. Other examples of the use of special funds include payment of certain rehabilitation benefits, payment of benefits in the case of an uninsured employer, and payment of certain benefits in the case of concurrent employment. As with second injury funds, unique forms of funding and administration have been developed for these special funds.

Chapter Nine Outline

I. Benefit Administration
    A. Benefit Administration
        1. Dissemination of Information
        2. Monitoring of the Benefit Delivery Process
        3. Rehabilitation and Medical Benefit Oversight
    B. Data Reporting
    C. Electronic Data Interchange (EDI)
    D. Benchmarking
    E. Types of Benchmarking

II. Dispute Resolution
    A. Informal Dispute Resolution
        1. Informal Resolution
        2. Mediation
        3. Non-Binding Arbitration
        4. Binding Arbitration
    B. Formal Dispute Resolution
        1. Administrative Appeals
        2. Appeals to the Judicial Level
    C. Alternate Dispute Resolution (ADR)
    D. Attorney Fees
    E. Lump Sum Settlements
        1. Commutations and Compromise Settlements

III. Special Funds
    A. Second Injury Funds
        1. Funding and Financial Growth
        2. State Efforts to Address Fund Growth
        3. Repeal of State Second Injury Fund Provisions
    B. Payment of Benefits for Uninsured Employers
    C. Payment of Supplemental Benefits
    D. Payment of Continuing Benefits on Time-Barred Claims
    E. Benefit Payments for Concurrent Employment
    F. Benefits During Rehabilitation and Job Modification
    G. Miscellaneous Situations

Chapter Nine Exercises

(Practice exercises are sample questions of material covered within each chapter)

1. What administrative functions are performed by a pro-active administrative agency?

2. How may a pro-active administrative agency provide assistance and guidance in the area of rehabilitation services?

3. What are some of the benefits associated with the introduction of electronic data interchange (EDI) for the administrative agency?

4. What are the three different types of informal dispute resolution? Briefly describe each.

5. In what ways does a formal dispute resolution process differ from an informal dispute resolution process?

6. What are some of the ways that attorney fees are established in the various states?

7. How does a "structured settlement" differ from a lump-sum settlement? What might some of the benefits of a structured settlement be for both the benefit recipient and the benefit administrator?

8. Describe the purpose and role of the original state second injury funds.

9. Why have a significant number of states taken steps to eliminate their second injury funds for newly arising cases?

10. What are some of the additional purposes that are afforded through state special funds that go beyond that of providing compensation in the case of a second injury?

CHAPTER TEN

THE RATE-MAKING PROCESS

Industry rating organizations play a crucial role in the determination of an employer's workers compensation premium. A rating organization is responsible for establishing an equitable and adequate classification for identifying and distinguishing between the different categories of employment. A rating organization is also responsible for collecting loss information detail for purposes of developing rates for the different employment classifications. Another role for the rating organization is to file rates with the individual states inasmuch as rates vary between states even for the same employment classification.

Under an insurance program, the employer is charged an annual premium for insurance coverage. Since companies and businesses are required to maintain payroll records for other purposes, and since these records are easily verified, the employer's payroll is generally considered as the measure of exposure for work-related injuries and disease.

The tool used in the majority of jurisdictions for premium calculation is the Basic Manual prepared by the National Council on Compensation Insurance (NCCI) - the insurance industry rating organization. The Basic Manual contains a listing of classifications, rates and rules applicable to both workers compensation and employers' liability insurance coverage. Employers are grouped into categories (classifications) based on the type of business the employer performs. While no two businesses are exactly alike, the classification system is based on the theory that similar businesses have similar risks along with similar types of loss exposure.

In the calculation of an employer's premium, the computation begins with the rate which is the amount of premium for each $100 of payroll. The premium for each classification shown in the policy is determined by multiplying the basis of premium by the rate. More than 600 different classifications are included in the Basic Manual along with a corresponding rate. The experience for each employment classification is determined and that computation serves as the "manual rate" for that classification. The manual rate is the average price for all employers in a particular classification and is an amount approved by the state department of insurance.

Workers compensation rates - or loss costs in a number of states - vary from state to state even within the same classification or type of business operation. This variation results from the level of benefits prescribed by a particular state along with the differences that may result from the different waiting periods that apply to the payment of income replacement benefits. The variation in rates or loss costs may also be the result of different loss experience as well as the expenses associated with individual states.

An employer's governing classification is that classification which describes the business. If the risk is subject to a single classification, that classification is the governing classification. In the case of a policy subject to more than one classification, the governing classification is that classification which develops the greatest amount of payroll.

The establishment and approval of manual rates for each classification represents the first step in the process. Within any one of the classifications - which include many risks – there will be varying hazard factors. This variation in hazard from risk to risk will depend upon factors such as the physical conditions of the workplace, the manner in which the product is manufactured, and the degree of the employer's attention to safety. This difference among risks within an individual classification prompted the establishment of some measurement of this variation in hazard. It was in this general way that the basic individual risk rating system – commonly referred to as the "experience rating plan" – evolved. Today, all risks in excess of a certain premium dollar threshold, that varies from state to state, are required to participate in the experience-rating program.

An experience rating plan attempts to measure the impact of the employer on the losses and rates the employer rather than the factory or building or equipment. The experience-rating plan determines whether a specific risk presents a hazard for future losses that is greater than or less than the hazard for the average risk. If the indication is that the risk is better than average, then there is a premium credit and the risk will pay less than the standard manual premium. On the other hand, if the risk is shown to have worse experience than average, the result will be a debit rating and the employer will pay more than the standard manual premium.

In contrast to the experience-rating plan, which is applied to the front-end of the rating process, there are a number of different loss sensitive programs designed to address the back-end of the rating process. The retrospective rating plan is an optional rating plan which modifies the premium for the existing policy on the basis of losses incurred during the policy period. This approach to rating serves to provide the insured employer with a premium that immediately reflects the character of the present losses. Retrospective rating plans are intended to operate as an incentive for the employer to control and reduce losses in order to reduce the amount of premium being charged.

Dividend plans are basically guaranteed cost plans that offer the potential for a financial reward if the employer has better than expected claims experience. Dividend plans typically base claim experience on the losses of a particular group to which the insured belongs or to an individual insured business. Dividend plans typically are reserved for those businesses that have better than average claim experience.

Deductible programs are a form of self-insurance which permits an employer to reimburse an insurance company for workers compensation losses, up to a stated deductible amount, in return for a lower premium. In states permitting the deductible program, the insurance company remains primarily liable for all claim payments and only following the payment of benefits is the insurer allowed to seek reimbursement from the insured employer.

Chapter Ten Outline

I. The Rate-Making Process
    A. Rating Organizations
    B. Functions of Rating Organizations
        1. The Classification System
        2. Collection of Statistical Data
        3. Filing for Rate Changes
        4. Manual Rates and Loss Costs
    C. Development of The Employer's Premium
        1. Remuneration Inclusions
        2. Remuneration Exclusions
        3. Other Considerations in Computing Remuneration
    D. Division of Payroll Rules
        1. Total Payroll Rule
        2. Payroll Limitation Rule
    E. Further Manual Rate Adjustments
        1. Minimum Premium
        2. Premium Discount
        3. Merit Rating
        4. Schedule Rating Credits or Debits
        5. Other Premium Credits or Debits
    F. Guaranteed Cost Plans
    G. Estimated Premium
    H. Premium Audits
    I. Other Policy Considerations

II. Experience Rating
    A. Characteristics of Experience Rating
    B. Experience In Modification Calculation
    C. Experience Modification Formula
        1. Primary and Excess Values
        2. Expected Loss Rate (ELR)
        3. Stabilizing Values
    D. Issuance of Experience Modification Factors

III. Loss Sensitive Programs
    A. Retrospective Rating Plans
        1. Basics of Retrospective Rating
        2. Retrospective Rating Formula
        3. Excess Loss Coverage
        4. Retrospective Development Factor
    B. Dividend Plans
    C. Deductible Programs

Chapter Ten Exercises

(Practice exercises are sample questions of material covered within each chapter)

1. What is a rating organization, and what are the primary functions or responsibilities served by a rating organization?

2. How does the classification system developed by the rating organizations differ from the occupational codes developed by the North American Industry Classification System (NAICS)?

3. How does the content of a loss cost filing differ from those of a manual rate filing?

4. How is the "governing classification" determined?

5. Describe the two primary benefits of experience rating.

6. Describe the role that "frequency" and "severity" play in the calculation of an experience modification factor. In your opinion, which factor – frequency or severity – is likely to be the better indicator of an employer's future potential loss experience?

7. List at least two ways in which the experience-rating plan differs from the retrospective rating plan.

8. What are the Basic Factor and the Loss Conversion Factor used in the calculation of retrospective premium?

9. Under what conditions are dividends paid?

10. What are the different types of small deductible programs permitted by the states?

CHAPTER ELEVEN

EXCLUSIVE REMEDY AND BAD FAITH

Before the first workmen's compensation laws were enacted, an injured worker, in order to recover damages for a work-related injury, was required to show some degree of fault on the part of the employer. Under what is now recognized as the *quid pro quo* of workers compensation law, employers are required to accept responsibility for injuries and death arising out of and in the course of employment without regard to the issue of fault. In exchange for these benefits, workers gave up the right to sue their employers for damages. These agreements are generally referred to as "exclusive remedy" provisions.

No rule is absolute, however. In virtually every state, injured workers are permitted to bring a direct action for damages against their employer where the employer has failed to purchase insurance coverage or qualify as a self-insurer. In addition, other exceptions to the exclusive remedy of workers compensation laws have developed over time. The most prevalent exceptions include:

> **Intentional tort or willful misconduct** – If an employer attacks or assaults an employee, the employer may be held responsible for injuries stemming from that assault. A number of jurisdictions (e.g., **Ohio** and **West Virginia**) have a rather protracted series of judicial decisions relative to the question as to what constitutes an intentional tort.
>
> **Intentional infliction of emotional distress** – While only a minority of states recognizes this theory of recovery against the employer, the courts often require outrageous conduct, clear harassment, or specific intent to cause an emotional disturbance.
>
> **Fraudulent concealment** – The exception to the exclusive remedy occurs when the employer learns of the existence of a workplace hazard (e.g., asbestos), which is causing harm to employees, but conceals the existence of the hazard and permits the employee to continue to suffer harm.
>
> **Dual capacity** – The dual capacity doctrine applies in the situation where the employer is acting in a "separate capacity" other than as the employer. Examples of claims in this category can stem either from medical care provided to an employee or where a product manufactured by the employer is the cause of an injury to an employee.
>
> **Third party action-over** – Typically, an injured employee may sue a manufacturer of the product that caused the workplace injury. In an action-over claim, the product manufacturer then impleads the employer under the theory of comparative negligence

or some similar theory of fault. The employer may then be held liable for a portion of any resulting award for damages.

Sexual harassment – A growing number of states are beginning to recognize sexual harassment as an exception to the exclusion remedy provision. This is generally driven by the fact that there is a strong public policy argument for permitting tort remedies for sexual harassment.

Retaliatory discharge - The majority of states recognize, either by case law or by statute, the tort of retaliatory discharge for filing a claim for workers compensation benefits. Even so, claims continue to be filed where employers let employees go following a workplace injury.

Loss of consortium - A claim for loss of consortium arises when one of the marriage partners has lost the companionship (consortium) of the other partner as the result of someone else's negligence or intentional conduct. Loss of consortium is broadly defined to include such things as the loss of society, affection, assistance, and the impairment of sexual relations in a marital relationship.

Included within the subject of exposure for injuries outside the scope of the law are those situations where claims to circumvent the exclusive remedy are prompted by the enactment by states of provisions designed to limit the scope of coverage or to further limit benefit entitlement.

Changes in statutory language regarding compensability standards (e.g., workplace event must be "major contributing cause") enacted by state legislatures beginning in the late 1980s, were designed to raise the threshold in terms of what constituted a compensable injury or occupational disease. A number of states have determined that where the alleged injury does rise to the level of the higher standard, the employee is free to bring an action for damages directly against the employer.

Many courts have ruled that the workers compensation carrier has a duty of "good faith and fair dealing" to the injured worker under the workers compensation policy in the same manner as to the named insured under any other insurance policy or contract. In a number of states, the courts have reasoned that subsequent to the workers compensation accident and injury, if the unreasonable claims handling causes additional pain, suffering, distress or damages in addition to the initial comp injury, the responsible party can be sued under a tort theory for knowingly, willfully, or recklessly inflicting injury or damage.

The workers compensation program in the various states operates efficiently so long as the participants are honest and operate in "good faith." Good faith requires the benefit payer to properly and timely investigate the claim and to pay benefits timely when due. When the payer fails or departs from that philosophy and the central purpose of the workers compensation program, is when problems arise which can result in fines, penalties, audits or bad faith claims.

Chapter Eleven Outline

I. Threats to the Exclusive Remedy
    A. Intentional Injury
        1. Specific Intent
        2. Employer Negligence
        3. Deliberate Intent
    B. Fraudulent Concealment
    C. Dual Capacity
        1. Employer Furnished Medical
        2. Employer Manufactured Products
        3. Legislative Response to Dual Capacity Actions
    D. Dual Persona
    E. Third Party Action Over
        1. Indemnification
        2. Contribution
            a. *Dole v. Dow*
            b. *Skinner v. Reed*
    F. Injury Outside Scope of Employment
        1. Mental Stress or Sexual Harassment
        2. Retaliatory Discharge
        3. Loss of Consortium
    G. Amended Compensability Standards
    H. Exposure for Non-Subscribers in Texas

II. Bad Faith and Unfair Claim Practices
    A. Avoiding Bad Faith
        1. Duty to Investigate
        2. Timely Payment of Benefits

Chapter Eleven Exercises

(Practice exercises are sample questions of material covered within each chapter)

1. What is the basis for the exclusive remedy provisions found in the workers compensation laws?

2. What is the public policy reason for permitting an exception to the exclusive remedy for intentional acts on the part of the employer?

3. What are the two different types of claims that can be brought under the "dual capacity doctrine?" Provide examples of each type.

4. What is a third-party action? Provide an example to illustrate a third party action-over.

5. What is meant by "indemnification" when involved with a third party action-over?

6. Under many early workmen's compensation laws, the exclusive remedy did not apply to injuries occurring outside the law. How did this early interpretation serve to broaden coverage under the compensation program?

7. What is meant by the term "loss of consortium?" What provision in the workers compensation law serves to preclude "loss of consortium" claims in the majority of states?

8. What is the significance of the Oregon Supreme Court decision in *Smothers v. Gresham*?

9. What is the significance in Texas of the Supreme Court ruling in Lawrence on the rights of injured workers, their employers, and the Texas workers compensation system as a whole?

10. What are the two principal elements of a "bad faith" claim?

Made in the USA
Columbia, SC
06 March 2020